A gift for:

From:

Drs. Les & Leslie Parrott

time together

meditations for your time-starved marriage

inspirio®

Contents

INTRODUCTION

Leslie and I recently celebrated our twentieth wedding anniversary over a nine-course dinner. We had never indulged in such an extravagant celebration before. The appetizer was served at 6:00 p.m. and the dessert arrived at our table near midnight. Never before had we lingered over such a lavish meal. And we do mean lingered. For nearly six hours, we sat at our cozy table with only the occasional interlude to roam through the restaurant's gardens to stretch our legs. Talk about "time together" — we had it in abundance. But don't think for a moment that this is a typical occasion in our marriage.

With two little ones at home — a busy six-year-old boy and an insatiable two-year-old boy — we relished every minute of our extraordinary escape as a couple. As anyone with small children knows, it's a palatable change of pace when you steal away as husband and wife.

Whew! As the hubbub of a fast-paced life morphs into a saner pace, you can almost feel yourself catching your breath. And, for some of us, it almost takes something as dramatic and unusual as a nine-course meal to slow us down. After all, if you're like us, you can get so caught up in your hurry-up pace that you become accustomed to rushing to and fro, forgetting what it's like to lavish your marriage with time. You may have been trying to save time and now find that you can't remember where all that time you saved has been stored.

Isn't that what all the fast pace is about? To save time? Who'd have thought that with all the technology designed to give us more time — the microwave ovens, the TiVo that lets us fast-forward, the

PalmPilots, the BlackBerrys — we'd be cramming all those "extra moments" we've saved with even more doing and less being? The truth is that, with all the gizmos and gadgets, we feel more frenzied, more harried, more out of breath than ever before.

That's why we wrote this little book of meditations. It's designed specifically for couples on the go, those who are looking for a tool to help them steal away — if only for a few minutes — and regain the moments they've been missing together.

As we were writing our book *The Time-Starved Marriage*, a more hard-hitting, roll-up-your-sleeves kind of book with dozens of tips, tests, and techniques for exploring each other's "time styles" (with workbook exercises and all the rest), we realized that a little book like the one you hold in your hands would be a natural companion. More contemplative. Reflective. Not so much a *study* in "how-tos" as it is an *experience* in having time together. We want you to read this at your own pace, a little at a time, as you're snuggled up on a couch or even in bed together.

You may choose to read from this book once a day or once a week, before you fall asleep or shortly after you get up in the morning. Regardless, we pray you will slow down, if only for the short time it takes to meditate on each one of these entries, and savor the time you have together.

With every good wish,
Les and Leslie Parrott
Seattle, Washington

Time Well Spent

Time is life. The way you spend your hours
and your days is the way you spend your life.

John Boykin

Recently a 1939 wristwatch giving the time in forty-two cities around the world was sold at auction for more than 6.6 million Swiss francs. That's 4 million U.S. dollars! The purchase doubled the world record for the sale price of a watch. The platinum "World Time" men's watch, made by Geneva manufacturer Patek Philippe, was sold to an unidentified buyer.

Can you imagine spending four million dollars on a watch? How about four thousand dollars? Four hundred? Okay — forty? We all know that the Timex you spent a few bucks on is going to keep time nearly as well as the Patek Philippe model, though maybe not in forty-two different cities around the world. So why would someone spend that kind of cash on such an exotic watch? Obviously, it's not about keeping time. It's about appreciating quality. It's about the fine art of timekeeping. It's about an investment. A significant investment.

The news of this extraordinary purchase got us to thinking about the value of our time as a couple and how we invest it. We began to wonder out loud about the time in our lives that's most valuable to us as husband and wife. And it didn't take us long to realize that the time that is most priceless to us is the time we have together. Certainly the time we spend at work is important and often fulfilling. The time we spend at church in worship with others is deeply meaningful. We thoroughly enjoy the time we have with friends. But the most valuable of all our time is the time we devote to our marriage and family. It's priceless. We wouldn't be tempted for a moment to trade it in on the platinum number from Geneva. And, because you're reading this little book we know you wouldn't be tempted either.

So the question is begging to be asked. What makes the time a husband and wife have together so extraordinarily valuable? You already know the answer. It's valuable because of the return on the investment. We don't know what the unidentified buyer of the fancy watch is going to get down the road, but we know exactly what we are going to get back as a result of the time we spend together: Love. The most valuable resource in the universe. We are going to get back compounded love on every memory we create.

Love is the *summum bonum* — the supreme good, the most excellent way. Love lifts us outside ourselves and allows us to see beyond the normal range of human vision. It inspires us to transcend who we are tempted to settle for. It defines us and shapes us into the person we were designed to be. No financial investment in the world can pay that kind of a dividend. And no marriage can ever reap the bountiful rewards of this love without the investment of time. It's a fact. To love and be loved you must spend time with the one you love. And as you do, love has the chance to compound.

Four million dollars is an impressive investment in a timepiece. No question about that. But it doesn't come close to what a husband and wife get out of time together. So as you meditate on the readings in this book, do so together. Consider each one an investment in your love bank. Linger when you can. Meander through these pages at your own pace and realize that the time you spend together is an investment in the quality of your marriage.

And consider this question: What's one specific difference you can each point to in your relationship when you have had time to connect — versus those days or weeks when time has been in short supply?

Whatsoever a man soweth, that shall he also reap.

 Galatians 6:7 KJV

Stop the Clock

Remember, people will judge you by your actions,
not your intentions. You may have a heart of gold —
but so does a hard-boiled egg.
Author Unknown

In the movie *The Patriot* starring Mel Gibson, we're reminded that
some things are worth fighting for.

It's 1776 in South Carolina when Gabriel Martin opens the door
of the church where a memorial service is in progress. Gabriel addresses Reverend Oliver, who is standing in the pulpit. "Reverend,
with your permission, I'd like to make an announcement."

Oliver replies, "Young man, this is a house of God."

Gabriel responds, "I understand that, Reverend, and I apolo-
gize. The South Carolina militia is being called up. I'm here to enlist
every man willing."

Oliver descends the stairs toward Gabriel and says, "Son, we are
here to pray for the souls of those men hanging outside."

Gabriel says, "Yes, pray for them but honor them by taking up
arms with us."

A man in the congregation stands to speak. "And bring more suffering to this town?"

Another man adds, "King George can hang those men, our friends. He can hang any one of us."

Anne Patricia Howard stands up and addresses the protester. "Dan Scott, barely a week ago, I heard you rail for two hours about independence." There is a stir among the congregation as she continues: "Mr. Hardwick, how many times have I heard you speak of freedom at my father's table? Half the men in this church, including you, Father, and you, Reverend, are as ardent patriots as I. Will you now, when you are needed most, stop only at words? Is that the sort of men you are?"

As the men reflect on her words, Anne continues, "I ask only that you act upon the beliefs of which you have so strongly spoken and in which you so strongly believe."

"Who's with us?" Gabriel asks.

One by one, the men and their sons stand in response to Anne Howard's challenge.

It's what we call a "stop the clock" moment. Time stands still as the human spirit ponders not what to say but what to do.

It's a moment when words are put into action and we summon the courage and the will to do what we believe is right.

Rhetoric, after all, comes easily. But not action. It's true in our marriages as well. Think of the words we uttered in our wedding vows. We can say them with great conviction but it's not until we truly love each other "in sickness and in health, for richer or poorer" that the words mean much.

So we ask you: What have you both been talking about that you haven't put into action? Is it a vacation getaway for just the two of you? Is it starting a class at your church for other couples? Is it instilling a routine date-night? Is it mentoring another couple? Maybe it's learning a new hobby together or simply making shared meal times a priority. It could be anything. What is it that you've been talking about but haven't done yet? Don't wait for a "stop the clock" moment to get you into action. Act upon your beliefs, as Anne Howard urged, and fight for your marriage. Don't just talk about it, do what you know will make it stronger.

Faith by itself, if it is not accompanied
by action, is dead....
I will show you my faith by what I do.

James 2:17 – 18

Another Year
Bites the Dust

The years run like rabbits.
W. H. Auden

Believe it or not, there's a website that allows you to enter your birth date and gender so that you can discover how much time you have left. Yikes! Known as the "Death Clock," it will instantly calculate the day you would die according to projections for the average life span. If you were born, say, on March 16, 1969, and are male, they say you'll have until December 26, 2042, based on an average life span. They'll also tell you that this is just 1.4 billion seconds away. Kind of crazy, don't you think? They bill themselves as the "the Internet's friendly reminder that life is slipping away."

Doesn't get much more macabre than that, but they're right. Time *is* slipping away. And there's nothing like a startling in-your-face reminder such as this website to make you take notice of its quick passage. And the older you get, the more you notice it. Each year seems to move more quickly than the last. As children, time sometimes felt like it was standing still, didn't it? But no longer. Consider an anonymous poet's ponderings on the passage of time.

When as a child, I laughed and wept,
Time crept.
When as youth, I dreamed and talked,
Time walked.
When I became a full-grown man,
Time ran.
And later, as I older grew,
Time flew.
Soon I shall find while traveling on,
Time gone.
Author Unknown

It may not be the most pleasant of thoughts, but an occasional reminder that our time on this planet is finite can awaken our appreciation for each and every moment we have. After all, nothing you can do will stop the march of time, but you can do plenty to make sure "the time you have left" is not wasted. It begins with paying attention to what makes your time on this earth so valuable to begin with. And, of course, that's your relationships. You may enjoy your home, your vacations, your work, or any other good fortunes, but everyone agrees that it is our relationships that give life meaning and fulfillment — especially our relationship with our soul mate.

So, as morbid as it might first seem, consider the days that you are likely to have left in this earthly life. Give serious thought to how you want to spend the days that stretch before you. Do you really have time to fuss and fight? Do you want to spend your time bellyaching and moaning? Do you want to give your very best at the office and only have what's leftover at home? Of course not. Nobody does.

We're all bound to have our share of conflict and busyness, but why let negativity steal the precious moments you have together? Instead, consider how you can curb whatever it is that tends to take time away from what you want most in your relationship and in this life you share together. Don't allow another year to bite the dust without squeezing the very life out of it.

Be careful how you live.
    Don't live like ignorant people,
but like wise people. Make good
    use of every opportunity you have.

Ephesians 5:15 – 16 GNT

Your Personal
Time Capsule

One of the truths about time capsules is that they are as much for the here and now as they are for the future.
Cathleen O'Connell

Tucked away in the corner of the basement of our house is a tightly wrapped box that has a simple handwritten sign affixed to it with a heavy dose of duct tape: "For John Parrott — to be opened on his sixteenth birthday." There's a similar box, also taped up with duct tape, beside it earmarked for John's little brother Jackson.

What do these homemade time capsules contain? A copy of the newspaper on the day each boy was born, their birth announcement, a letter from Mom and Dad, and about a half dozen trinkets, photos, and memorabilia that are sure to generate conversation for a sixteen-year-old boy when he opens it on his birthday.

There's something about leaving a message and some artifacts for future delivery that intrigues the human spirit. And time capsules aren't just kids stuff. Instant archeology has been created by civic groups, schools, churches, and businesses for eons. The first such capsule of note in America was the dream of a Civil War widow, Mrs. Charles

Deihm. At the Philadelphia Centennial Exhibition of 1876, Mrs. Deihm closed up some commemorative items in a "century safe" to be opened in 1976. Right on time, President Ford duly unsealed it, and from its purple velvet interior removed a watch, a tea service, and a few leather-bound books.

Few institutions could resist the temptation of marking their new skyscrapers with the ritual of a time capsule. The daughter of the *New York Times'* publisher, Iphigene Ochs Sulzberger, buried a time capsule in the Times Tower in 1904 and was on hand to open it in 1964, retrieving the obligatory coins and newspapers. The Pulitzers also socked away a time capsule in their 1884 tower in Manhattan.

In 1977, "Sounds of Earth," a two-disc record set was strategically mounted on the Voyager 2 spacecraft. The gold discs — which include recordings of Chuck Berry, Mozart, and a human kiss — come with a cartridge, a needle, and instructions for playing them. Who knows what future generations or aliens will discover this treasure.

Regardless of whether the capsule is actually retrieved or not, it's a pretty good exercise to consider what you might put in it. That's why we want to suggest you consider a time capsule for your marriage. Whether you actually build one or not, consider what you might put into your time capsule. If it were to be opened in one hundred years by your grandchildren and great-grandchildren and you wanted them to know about your relationship, what would you place in your time capsule? What artifacts would you want them to see and talk about as it relates to your marriage? It's a useful exercise. One that may help you be more intentional about your marital legacy.

While you're at it, what would you place in a time capsule to be opened on your fiftieth wedding anniversary? Do any artifacts come to mind? How about a simple letter from each of you to the other that won't be read until that day?

A scroll of remembrance
was written in his presence
concerning those who feared the
LORD and honored his name.

Malachi 3:16

What Time Is It?

He who neglects the present moment
throws away all he has.
Johann Friedrich von Schiller

What's the very first thing you do when you wake up each morning? What's the first thing you want to know? Think about it. Everyone of us wakes up with the same question on our mind: What time is it? That's why we check the clock the moment our eyes open. It's the same clock we looked at just before we fell asleep.

It's a good question: *What time is it?* Not only because the question helps us stay on schedule but if you ask it from a more contemplative place, as in what time is it in my life, it can really give you pause. In other words the question becomes, what time is it right now for me (regardless of what the clock says)? It is time for you to recharge your batteries? Time to take care of an errand that's long overdue? Time to phone a friend you've neglected? In other words, what time is it, really?

It's the kind of question that keeps us fully present — right now. Too often, you see, we get dragged down by the past, wallowing in regret about yesterday, or pulled forward by the future, dreaming of what might be tomorrow. And either way we can be swayed from living fully in the here and now. And that's what time it is! *It's now.*

We have a friend who doesn't wear a watch because he says it doesn't matter what time the watch says, what matters is that the time is now. We've never figured out how he makes his appointments but you can't argue that his philosophy is true. Right now is what matters most.

Our friend John Maxwell, in his book *Today Matters*, says, "It may sound trite, but today is the only time you have. It's too late for yesterday. And you can't depend on tomorrow. That's why today matters." We couldn't agree more. And we've seen John live out this principle with Margaret, his wife, on many occasions. John is one of the most conscientious timekeepers we've ever met. He milks every moment, wanting to bring Margaret into his life at every turn. Sure, he plans for the future and he ponders the past, but make no mistake that John lives for the moment.

You can too. Why? Because it's a choice. Being fully present is the result of deciding to be mindful of what this hour holds. It's being conscious of the fact that yesterday ended last night and tomorrow hasn't arrived. What you have is now. That's all you can be certain of so decide to use it.

Every once in a while you ask someone what they are doing and they say "I'm just killing time." Think about that. They might as well say "I'm throwing away my life." The time we have in the here and now is the only time within our grasp. As Alice Bloch said, "We say we waste time, but that is impossible. We waste ourselves."

The very fact that you are reading these words, consciously focusing on how to best use your time together, tells us that you are light-years ahead of other couples in practicing this principle. But if you are like us, you can always benefit from being reminded to be more mindful of being fully present in the moment. So, what can you do in your relationship this week, specifically, to do just that? How can you help each other live fully in the moment when you are together?

Here's a little tip that's helped us. When one of us is either wallowing in the past or living for tomorrow, we ask a simple question: What time is it? Of course, the other will quickly scan for the clock. Then we'll ask it again: What time is it, really?

Sounds goofy, but this little exercise is usually all it takes to snap us back into the moment and remember that now is all we have. And that's enough.

This is the day the LORD has made;
let us rejoice and be glad in it.

Psalm 118:24

This Could Be a Long Conversation

Marriage is one long conversation, chequered by disputes.
Robert Louis Stevenson

The monks at a remote monastery deep in the woods followed a rigid vow of silence. Their vow could only be broken once a year — on Christmas — by one monk. That monk could speak only one sentence. One Christmas, Brother Thomas had his turn to speak and said, "I love the delightful mashed potatoes we have every year with the Christmas roast!" Then he sat down. Silence ensued for 365 days.

The next Christmas, Brother Michael got his turn and said, "I think the mashed potatoes are lumpy, and I truly despise them!" Once again, silence ensued for 365 days.

The following Christmas, Brother Paul rose and said, "I am fed up with this constant bickering!"

We chuckle at the very thought of this but truth is that some couples can carry on a conflict that will last nearly as long. In our book *Love Talk* we devote an entire chapter to "When Not to Talk." It may seem a bit unorthodox that in a communication book we are telling our readers to stop talking, but let's be honest. Some conversations simply don't need to take place. They waste our time.

If you've been telling your husband for eight years to not put his jacket on the back of the dining room chair and he's still doing it, or you've been arguing for four summers about whether or not to buy an expensive barbeque grill, it might be time to take a permanent break from the conversation. At some point you've got to realize that talking is not going to provide the solution.

If you've locked horns on replacing your washer and dryer or on how much money to give to a charitable cause, you might simply have to agree to disagree. You may be able to work out a compromise that will at least partly satisfy you both. Or maybe you go on as you have been and agree to table all discussion on the matter for, say, the next six months.

The point is that if your conversations are getting you nowhere, you need to give it a rest and reclaim the time you've been wasting on them. Of course, in some cases, there are actions you can take that *do* speak louder than words. If you've asked, cajoled, threatened, and analyzed your man on the subject of not hanging up his coat in the closet, and he keeps promising to do so but never does, you have some options.

(a) You could decide to hang it up for him and say no more about it.

(b) You could leave it there and say nothing.

(c) You could hide his jacket each time he leaves it in an undesirable spot.

This last option is for those with a mean streak (we don't recommend it), but we want to give you all the options here. The only option not available to you is to keep talking about it.

The bottom line is that you need to give up the conversations you keep having over and over and over. They will grind both of you down and steal precious time from talks that could be much more meaningful. So take a moment to identify what one of those "long conversations" might be for each of you.

Say only what will help to build others up and meet their needs. Then what you say will help those who listen.

Ephesians 4:29 NIrV

Time Is Money

Time is the coin of your life. It is the only coin you have,
and only you can determine how it will be spent.
Be careful lest you let other people spend it for you.
Carl Sandburg

How much money would you need to improve your life? Go
ahead — think about this. Talk it over with each other. After all, nearly
everyone, no matter how much money they have, would like more — be-
lieving that it would ease their angst or improve their happiness. So
what about you? How much would it take to really make a difference
in your life?

Got a figure in mind? Let's see how you stack up with other
people.

When asked how much money it would take to make a real difference in their lives, 33 percent of people say that an extra $100,000
in the bank would improve their lot, and 14 percent would want up
to $500,000. An even million would shake things up, say 16 percent,
and 24 percent calculate it would take up to $10 million. Seems we're
all over the map when it comes to feeling financially fit, which makes
sense because money, like time, is relative.

One of the supreme lessons in life seems to be that the less time you
have on this earth, the more likely you are to give your money away.

And these days, according to a recent *Newsweek* article, there's a new breed of givers known as "engaged philanthropists." Kenneth Behring is a good example. He seemed to have everything. He was affluent and generous. But something transformed him during a trip to Vietnam in 2000. The retired construction magnate was helping a relief organization bring food and medicine to a village. It was there Behring personally delivered a wheelchair to a six-year-old polio victim. The girl's reaction changed his life.

"She got a big smile on her face. She couldn't believe it," said Behring. "It's a sensation I've never experienced with anything else." Inspired, Behring, who used to donate time and money to other charities, created the Wheelchair Foundation, which today delivers ten thousand wheelchairs a month worldwide.

More of today's philanthropists are no longer satisfied with making a charitable donation. They want to see how the money is put to use and perform the benevolence themselves. They choose hands-on involvement over writing checks.

You don't have to be a wealthy benefactor to give with a hands-on approach. In fact, it doesn't matter how much money you have, giving is good for your marriage. We know that agreeing on financial matters in marriage is not always easy. It can be an emotional proposition.

We certainly don't always see eye-to-eye on finances in our home. But a fundamental shift of attitude toward giving took place when we changed the question we were asking of each other. Rather than "How much of our money should we give to God?" we learned to ask, "How much of God's money should we spend on ourselves?" The difference between these two questions was monumental for us. With this under-standing — that our income is all God's — as a starting point, we eliminated much of the legalistic thinking and guilt related to giving based on a set percentage of income. John Wesley understood this when he said, "Gain all you can, save all you can, give all you can."

Only 13 percent of the population believes money can buy happiness. But almost everyone believes that giving generously to others brings great joy. And it does. Add to that the element of a husband and wife participating together and that joy is multiplied. So consider how the two of you might spend some time doing a little hands-on helping. It may be one the most important investments you ever make in your marriage.

Be generous:
            Invest in acts of charity.
      Charity yields high returns.

Ecclesiastes 11:1 MSG

No Time for Sex? Really?

When you're deeply absorbed in what you're doing, time
gives itself to you like a warm and willing lover.

Brendan Francis

"Tell me," said David Letterman, to an actor he was interviewing on his
late night talk show, "you're a sex symbol who plays all sorts of exciting
roles with gorgeous women. How does that compare to your real life,
offscreen?"

The actor reminded Letterman that he had been happily married
for twenty years. Then he said, "Here's the difference in a nutshell. In
the movies, life is mostly about sex and occasionally about children.
Married life is mostly about children and occasionally about sex."

Our friends David and Claudia Arp once wrote a book for married couples called *No Time for Sex*. "It's a complaint we are hearing from
more and more couples," Claudia told us. "They are so busy running
the rat race that when they fall into bed, that's about all they can do."

And she's right. We hear the same complaint at our marriage semi-
nars around the country. Strange isn't it. After all, making love is something that most couples rank very high on their list of favorite activities. According to more than one recent survey reported in *USA Today*,
one of women's favorite home activities is "spending time with family,"

chosen by 65 percent of respondents. Next was listening to music (47 percent) but next in line was making love (46 percent). It may not surprise you to know that men, on the other hand, ranked "making love" as their very first favorite home pursuit (64 percent). Spending time with family was second (56 percent).

So why aren't couples finding the time for one of the activities they enjoy the most? Perhaps German philosopher Soren Kierkegaard hinted at the answer when he said, "Most [people] pursue pleasure with such breathless haste that they hurry past it." Could it be? In our fast pace, could we be failing to savor the scintillating pleasure of making love as husband and wife? Could we be cutting the corners on the delectable delight?

The answer is yes. At the end of a long day, most couples are too worn-out for sex. Working fewer hours is one way to free up energy and time for sex, which is why couples make love more often on vacation. But fatigue and time pressure are not the only reasons for having a sex-starved marriage. According to Carl Honore, author of *In Praise of Slowness*, "Our hurry-up culture teaches that reaching the destination is more important than the journey itself — and sex is affected by the same finishing-line mentality."

We can hear some of you saying that speed has its place between the sheets. Long live "the quickie." Sure. But making love slowly can be a profound experience. Some soft music, a few candles, and plenty of time for gentle caresses are sure to join your spirits and slow down your souls. Not to mention that it will extend your pleasure.

So if you've been rushing through the bliss of married sex, slow down. There's no need to hurry. Taking your time to make love to each other is some of the most important time that a husband and wife ever spend. Make it last.

May your fountain be blessed,
     and may you rejoice in the wife of your youth.
A loving doe, a graceful deer—
     may her breasts satisfy you always,
     may you ever be captivated by her love.

Proverbs 5:18–19

Tic-Talk a Lot

When I think of talking, it is of course with a woman.
For talking at its best being an inspiration, it wants a
corresponding divine quality of receptiveness,
and where will you find this but in a woman?
Oliver Wendell Holmes

One of the most famous time pieces on television has appeared every Sunday night for decades. The hard-hitting *60 Minutes* newsmagazine's stopwatch has been ticking away since the day it first aired on September 24, 1968. Well, almost. The actual timepiece is in the Smithsonian.

TV News magazine reports that the first watch, a Minerva, was used for only a few editions, then it was replaced by a Heuer. The familiar one, an Aristo, began to appear in the late 1970s and still remains as the template for the current stopwatch symbol.

To create the stopwatch visual for the many years of the program before computer graphics, the physical watch would be attached to a stand. "With the camera rolling, the watch would sometimes fall off its stand, to which it had once been applied with tape, and later, Velcro," said one television historian. "Or sometimes people forgot to wind it, so it would stop. Other times, flies would choose the worst times to land on its shiny surface."

Regardless of when and how it was produced for the show, that stopwatch with the notable sound of its "tic … tic … tic …" is synonymous with some of the most scintillating news stories on television. We've watched the program, the most successful broadcast in television history, for years and it almost always generates a healthy discussion in our home.

We can talk for long periods about the shady diploma mill Mike Wallace uncovered. Or the inexplicable streak of genius displayed by a savant in a story from Morley Safer. And whether he makes us smile or makes us mad, Andy Rooney is hard to ignore. Like we said, the program almost always gets us talking.

And that's the point. Talking. Did you know that communication is the very lifeblood of your relationship? And yet it is the number-one complaint most couples have about their relationship. "We just don't communicate," is a common refrain in many counselors' offices. Or "We never have time just to talk" is one we hear a lot. But the one that makes us cringe the most is "When we finally find the time to talk, we don't have anything to say."

Whether a relationship sinks or swims depends on how well a husband and wife send and receive messages, how well they use their conversations to understand and be understood. Think about it. If you are feeling especially close to your partner, it is because you are communicating well. Your spirits are up. Your love life is full. You are in tune. And when communication falls flat, when you feel stuck and you're talking in circles, relational satisfaction drops. As we said in our recent book *Love Talk*, communication, more than any other aspect of your relationship, can either buoy relational intimacy or be the dead-weight of its demise.

That's why this aspect of your relationship can always benefit from an infusion of time. Time and talk are always a winning combination. A good conversation simply doesn't happen while traveling at breakneck speed. Experts agree that most couples need a good sixty minutes each day to converse. Lingering over the evening meal can often serve this purpose. For some couples it means taking advantage of a quiet house when the kids are in bed. Or maybe turning off the radio when you are driving together in the car, or turning off the TV when it is simply background noise — so you can talk.

You get the idea. Oh, and one more practical way to eliminate hurry from your conversations? Drop this sentence from your personal lexicon: "Get to the point."

Enough said.

They devoted
themselves to ... fellowship.

Acts 2:42

Second Chances

Grace is given not because we have done good works,
but in order that we may be able to do them.
Saint Augustine

The old-fashioned western *Open Range* is about a confrontation
over land rights between free-ranging cowboys and a land-owning
rancher. But it's also about second chances — especially the kind a
husband or wife can offer each other. When the rancher kills cowboy
Charley Waite's friends, Charley, played by Kevin Costner, returns to
the rancher's town to seek justice and revenge.

His plans for bloodshed, however, reawaken memories of the Civil
War. As an assassin, he had killed hundreds, and as the war grew long,
he stopped discriminating between soldiers and civilians, between men,
women, and children. He had killed them all.

But when Charley meets Sue Barlow, played by Annette Bening,
Charley sees the possibility of a different life for himself — a life filled
with love, home, and family. Until he met Sue, Charley considered such
a life out of reach for a man with his murderous past. Yet, Sue's love
calls him to that different life.

Charley's violent side reemerges in a shootout in which he is wounded. He resolves to leave Sue and his dreams of a changed life. As Charley prepares to leave, Sue tells of her patient love for him, despite his past.

In a dusty, shot-up saloon, Sue tells him, "I don't have the answers, Charley, but I know that people get confused in this life about what they want, and what they've done, and what they think they should have done because of it. Everything they think they are or did takes hold so hard that it won't let them see what they can be."

She continues, "I've got a big idea about us, Charley ... and I'm not going to wait forever, but I am going to wait. And when you're far away, I want you to think about that ... and come back to me."

And he does.

Love, infused with patience, will almost always pass the test of time. That's the meaning of grace. Few acts on this planet are more grace-full than that of waiting on and loving a husband or wife who is still in process. And aren't we all. Who among us has arrived? Each and every one of us is in need of patient grace from our spouse.

And so we ask you, not where are you giving grace to each other — no need to instill guilt. The more poignant question is, where do you need grace from your partner today? Once you begin to answer this question, the more likely you are to receive it. Humility engenders grace in a marriage. It cultivates patient love. So we'll ask it again: Where and how do you most need grace from your spouse? Can you talk about this with each other?

Dwight L. Moody said, "Grace is love that cares and stoops and rescues." Where do you need to be cared for most? Where do you need your spouse to stoop down with you and offer mercy?

And as you both attempt to muster up grace within you to give each other, we want to pass along a tip that has helped us when pride keeps us from offering patient and merciful love to each other. Simply take that behavior, that trait, that bad habit, that thing that irritates you or angers you and say, "There but for the grace of God go I."

Be kind and compassionate to one another, forgiving each other, just as in Christ God forgave you.

Ephesians 4:32

Wait Just a Minute

Waiting is a period of learning.
Henri Nouwen

A man and woman spotted each other on the morning New York to Washington air shuttle. Sparks flew, but no words were exchanged, even as they stood together in the taxi line at Washington National. She got in a cab, looked back, and saw him running after her. She begged the cabbie to stop, but he kept going. In desperation, she scrawled her phone number on a piece of paper and pressed it against the back window. But she knew the man was too far away to read it.

So she went to her meeting. But she couldn't stop thinking about him. So she feigned illness and returned to the airport to wait for him to catch the shuttle back to New York. She waited all day and got on the 9:00 p.m. flight alone.

In New York, dejected, she stepped into the gate area — and he was there. "What took you so long?" he asked. "I've been waiting all day."

According to Dini Von Mueffling in her book *The 50 Most Romantic Things Ever Done*, the couple married and have two children. Whether this is an urban myth or a true story, it reveals the sage advice of the pithy proverb: Good things come to those who wait. And they do.

Eugene Peterson's paraphrase of Romans 8:22 – 25 resonates with Nouwen: "Waiting does not diminish us, any more than waiting diminishes a pregnant mother. We are enlarged in the waiting" (The Message). Of course, this is particularly true of couples in marriage. As we learn to wait on each other, our own character is built in the process. And as we wait on something together as a couple, our relationship matures. It builds endurance and we learn to share a sense of delayed gratification.

Of course, few of us enjoy waiting. We tend to be impatient and restless. Waiting seems like a waste of time. Yet when we wait we often reap a reward. The famed perfume and cosmetic mogul Estée Lauder can attest to that. Shortly after starting her business, she realized she had to persuade a cosmetics buyer to place her products in many stores throughout the country. At 9:00 a.m., Lauder was in the offices of the American Merchandising Corporation, waiting to see Marie Weston, the cosmetics buyer. Since Lauder had no appointment, she was advised to come back another day.

"I don't mind waiting," said Lauder. "I'll wait until she has a few free moments."

Salespeople came and went. At lunch time, the receptionist said Weston's schedule was so full that getting to see her was impossible. Again, Lauder was told to come back later.

"I'll wait a little longer," she persisted.

Hours passed. At 5:15 p.m. Marie Weston came out of her office. She looked at Estée Lauder in disbelief, then admiration, and said, "Well, do come in. Such patience must be rewarded."

Weston was impressed with Lauder's cosmetics, but there was no room in any of the stores. Come back later, she was encouraged. Of course, Estée did. Eventually, Weston found room in several stores. Business began to boom. The Estée Lauder name became famous in the world of cosmetics.

So what are the two of you waiting for? Chances are you know the answer to this question immediately. Maybe it's a job promotion or a raise in salary. Maybe the slow grief of a lost loved one to dissipate. Perhaps it's an upcoming vacation or a new life phase, like enjoying an empty nest. Or maybe it's the arrival of a new baby. Most of us, most of the time are waiting for something. And that's why a prayer for patience is always in order. Have you asked God to give you this gift in your marriage lately?

If we hope for what we do not yet have, we wait for it patiently.

Romans 8:25

Get Ready for Time Travel

Out testing time machine, be back yesterday.
Donald Duck

A newlywed couple returned from their honeymoon and set up house. On the first morning in their new home together, the wife decided to make her husband breakfast as a special treat. She fried up some eggs, made toast, and poured him a big cup of coffee. She hadn't done much cooking in her life, and she hoped he would be pleased by her effort, but after taking a few bites he said, "It's just not like Mom used to make."

She tried not to let his comment hurt her feelings, and since she wanted their life together to start on a positive note, she determined to get up the next morning and try again. Once again she got up early, prepared a meal, and put it in front of her husband. And again, his response was, "It's just not like Mom used to make."

Two more times she made him breakfast, and two more times she got the same response. Finally, she was fed up. The next morning, she cooked two eggs until they were as hard as rubber. She incinerated some bacon. She kept putting the bread back in the toaster until it turned black. And she cooked the coffee until it was like mud.

When her husband came to the table, she put his food in front of him, and she waited. The man sniffed the coffee, took one look at his plate, and said, "Hey! "It's just like Mom used to make!"

Seems silly, but there's a profound truth in this story: The home we grew up in shaped forever our expectations and desires. Not all of them, grant you, but many of our fundamental and quirky expectations stem from yesteryear. That's why it can always be a valuable exercise for every couple to embark on some time travel with each other.

Can you imagine if you had a time machine that enabled you to go back to your spouse's childhood and quietly observe him or her at home, at school, and with friends? Can you imagine the tremendous insight you would have into his or her being? We think you'd be amazed to discover the answers to an endless string of questions you've had about why he or she behaves in certain ways at certain times. You'd be shocked to discover how much easier it is to empathize with your spouse — to see the world from his or her perspective — after returning from this time travel. Why? Because you would understand more deeply than ever before what your spouse's life was like. You would have witnessed the times he was chided by his father or the times he was befriended by a classmate. You'd have seen her when she was most lonely or when she felt most proud. By stepping into his or her formative years you would now see your spouse from a whole new angle.

Of course, technology shows no signs of enabling couples to enjoy the benefits of such time travel, but that doesn't need to keep us from catching a glimpse of a few scenes from your spouse's childhood. Here's what you can do. Set aside some time in the coming days to devote an hour or so to visiting each other's childhoods. Each of you can pull together photos (maybe even home movies) and memorabilia about your life as a child. Start with your earliest memory and travel through your elementary school years. Explore not only what happened along this formative timeline but talk about how you felt and what you thought during your most vivid memories. Ask each other questions about important relationships.

We know you've already done this by virtue of being married, but you've probably never done so with such intention. Of course, the choice is yours, but no matter how long you've known each other, we guarantee you that this little time-travel trip is sure to bring new insight and ultimately bring you closer together.

Call out for the ability to be wise.
Cry out for understanding.
Look for it as you would look for silver.
Search for it as you would search for hidden treasure.

Proverbs 2:3–4 NIrv

If I Could Turn Back Time

Don't let yesterday use up too much of today.
Will Rogers

Thrifty Car Rental sponsors an annual Honeymoon Disasters Contest, and they have received stories on everything from mud slides to Montezuma's revenge.

For example, on their way to Nevada, Paul and Leah Lusk of Sugar City, Idaho, flipped their car into floodwaters. When they emerged, Paul, who had hit his head, couldn't remember the accident, recognize his bride, or recall he'd just been married.

Then there is the story of Chris and Doug of Clovis, California, who honeymooned in Cancun, Mexico. They lounged by the pool, ate terrific seafood buffets, and went dancing. Back at the hotel, six-foot-three, 255-pound Doug playfully threw his bride on the bed. He landed on her and broke two bones in her right leg. Three hours, one plate, and eight screws later, Chris was left with an $11,000 hospital bill that insurance wouldn't cover.

Mae and Kyle of Richmond, Virginia, who were finalists in Thrifty's contest last year, were forced to listen to the comedian on their cruise ship joke about the Titanic movie. Then the couple awoke to the horrible sound of crunching metal and the captain's order to abandon ship. Their lifeboat made it to shore in St. Marten, where the cruise line put them up at a nudist colony.

If there were ever any couples who wish they could turn back time it would have to be these poor souls. But truth be told, don't all of us wish we could do that on occasion. Don't you have a few conversations with each other you'd like to do over? Doors of opportunity you never opened and wished you would have? Decisions about finances you'd redo? We certainly would. Who wouldn't?

After all, everyone has at least a few regrets. Some major some minor. As Garrison Keillor says, "Show me a person without regret, and I'll show you a person with memory loss."

Because we've seen some couples poison their lives with regret while others have used it to propel them to a better way of living, we felt compelled to breach the subject with you. The former spend their days punishing themselves for something they didn't do or feel they should have done differently: "If only I'd checked the weather report before we left home," they say. "If only I would have set better boundaries with my in-laws." "If only I would have torn up our credit cards before we got into this kind of debt." "If only ..." Whether it's over the road not taken or the one taken too long, "if onlys" can hound a couple to death.

Then there are those couples who have suffered significant pain in their past — overcoming everything from angry words to bankruptcy or worse — and somehow risen above it. They've wrestled their regrets to the ground and walked away victorious. They no longer allow their yesterdays to use up their todays.

The point is that either your past is serving as a springboard to a better tomorrow, or it is the proverbial albatross keeping you from moving forward today. The choice is yours. What shouldas, couldas, and wouldas do you both need to surrender? Once you begin to talk them through with each other, it will help you release the power they have on you and you'll be amazed at how much time you find in your present when you feel freed from your past.

Forgetting what is behind and straining toward what is ahead, I press on toward the goal to win the prize for which God has called me heavenward in Christ Jesus.

Philippians 3:13 – 14

Stop and Smell the Spices

A smiling face is half the meal.
Latvian Proverb

Three nights a week, Kristi and Roger Strode turn the lights low, put on soft music, and sit down to eat by candlelight. This isn't a romantic dinner. It's supper with the kids.

The Strodes have three children, two jobs, and very little time. Until a few months ago, they described their family dinners as "gang grabs": everyone reaching for their own thing — frozen waffles, peanut butter, a bowl of cereal — and gobbling it down on the fly. But dinner in their Shorewood, Wisconsin, household has been transformed with the introduction of the candles, music, and one simple, cooked meal for everyone. "There's real conversation now and less bickering," Ms. Strode told Hilary Stout of the *Wall Street Journal*. "It brings the whole energy level down to a good place."

It's difficult to exaggerate the value of sharing a slow-paced family meal together. Study after study finds that kids who eat dinner with their families regularly are better students, healthier people, and less likely to smoke, drink, or use drugs than those who don't. It's enough to make you sprint to set the table.

But be assured, the benefits of lingering over a meal go far beyond the kids. A husband and wife are guaranteed to draw their spirits together when they instill table time for meals as a common practice. Why? Because there's something about breaking bread together at the end of the workday that is instantly bonding. Sure, it takes preparation time and you're bound to run into logistical challenges involving schedules, but the effort is worth it. Don't allow yourselves to become daunted by doing dinner together. If you find the kids are squabbling more than sharing around the table, Dr. Bill Doherty, professor of family social science at the University of Minnesota, has some suggestions.

First, he advises, ask yourself: "What am I doing that makes it worse?" The answer in many cases is unnecessary reprimanding. The classic "no dessert unless you behave and eat" turns dinner into a control struggle, which defeats the purpose. If they don't eat their vegetables, he suggests, let it go.

Also, don't turn the conversation into an interrogation session about school or activities. A more off-the-wall conversation starter might get everyone engaged. One of his suggestions: If you could meet someone from history, who would it be?

A little more creativity may be in order to keep smaller kids seated. Try a one-color meal — everything green might even help in the "eat your vegetables" department. Or an alphabet dinner, with every dish beginning with the same letter (pasta with plums and pears). Get them excited by picnicking in the living room one night or even eating under the table. You get the idea. If you have little ones, be creative and don't let that stop you from enjoying the benefits that come from spending time together over a meal.

And if dinner is simply too much to handle, try breakfast. Or start with just one night a week. Most important, Mr. Doherty says: "Make it special. Light candles, put a tablecloth out." In other words, make a distinction between a routine meal and a meaningful family ritual. A mealtime ritual is a keystone for finding time together.

> Your wife will be like a fruitful vine
> within your house;
> your sons will be like olive shoots
> around your table.

Psalm 128:3

Sleepy Time

Sleep is the golden chain that ties
health and our bodies together.

Thomas Dekker

Not so many years ago, women's magazines encouraged readers to set
the alarm half an hour earlier in order to find quiet time alone or to get
more done. Dark raccoon circles under your eyes from too many short
nights? Not to worry. The solution became, not more sleep, but artfully
applied makeup known as "concealer." Now the same publications are
running headlines touting the value of sleep.

It seems that sleep is in. It's the new luxury — for those that have
the time.

As one sign of changing attitudes toward sleep, the Sealy Company is spending an estimated $20 million on print and television ads
to emphasize the value of a good night's sleep. It also wants to change
its image from being a mattress company to that of a "sleep-wellness
provider."

Even airlines are marketing sleep, albeit at hefty prices. In some
first-class cabins on international flights, seats turn into full-length
beds. For thousands of dollars, pampered executives can sleep like a

baby at thirty-nine thousand feet, while the rest of us back in the sardine section sit upright, struggling to get even an hour's rest.

The corporate world also is beginning to catch on. A handful of companies now provide nap rooms, recognizing that a midday snooze can improve a worker's alertness. And in many hotels, sleep has become the new status symbol. Westin advertises a "Heavenly Bed," offering "layers of comfort and relaxation." And certain Hilton Hotels feature "Sleep-Tight" rooms, complete with soundproofing, special drapes, and other sleep aids. A special promotion allowed guests in those rooms to even take their pillows home with them.

Truth be told, however, the perfect bed is not simply about sheets and pillows. It's about the relationship of the husband and wife who sleep on them. It's about the tone they set in the late-night hours as they are dozing off to sleep, side by side. More important than the quality of the linens is the quality of the relationship. And the time we spend as a couple in bed talking about the residue of the day and our plans for tomorrow — our pillow talk — becomes some of the most important and precious moments in marriage. Even if you don't happen to go to bed at the same time, the person who turns in earlier can invite the other partner to share a few minutes together.

The time you have for pillow talk — when you are by nature slowing down, breathing deeper, and relaxing your muscles — should never be taken for granted. It's too good of an opportunity to let it go unnoticed.

Did you know your pillow talk can dramatically determine your dreams? It can also influence how well you sleep, and how you feel when you wake up in the morning. So don't waste this time. When you hit the hay tonight take a moment to savor the change in your pace. Notice your body's desire to lean into this antidote to stress and hurry. Talk to each other about your busy day. What was your high and low? And check in with each other on how you can pray for the upcoming day.

Savor the time before you fall asleep. It's the perfect time to rejoin your spirits.

If two lie down together,
they will keep warm

Ecclesiastes 4:11

Measuring Time ...
by Its Purpose

I learned to tell time and now I'm always late.

Lilly Tomlin

Ever heard of horology? Briefly, it's the science of measuring time and it has been around, well, a long time. It started back in the days of the Babylonians who came up with the idea for the sixty-second minutes and sixty-minute hours we use now. These days, horology is in the hands of scientists who go to great lengths to accurately measure miniscule moments in time. They literally measure time in billionths of a second by using atomic clocks. Horology has come a long way.

The first timekeeping device was probably a stick in the ground, and some clever soul noticed that the stick's shadow moved as the sun moved. From that came the present sundial. Another device was the water clock, in which a bowl was either filled or emptied within a certain period of time, probably timed by the shadow of a stick in the ground — but you could use the water clock at night. Other devices were marked candles, oil lamps that would burn a measured amount of oil, or a stick of incense that burned at a measured rate and would drop a thread-suspended, metal ball on a bell.

One of the first mechanical clocks — an alarm clock — was made by a blacksmith in Italy for a brother in a monastery who had to wake his mates at a certain time of the morning to start the day's worship sequence. From this sprang the monster tower clocks, again made by blacksmiths, which appeared all over Europe after about 1200. These only had one hand because they were so inaccurate — maybe within two hours a day.

The first watch appeared in about 1500. Not very accurate but a toy for the wealthy. Over the centuries, with the invention of the hair spring and other improvements, it became more accurate and smaller until it evolved into the small jewel you wear on your wrist today.

You may not be a horologist, but you are, no doubt, interested in measuring time. You have a watch to wear and several clocks in your home, right? But when it comes to measuring time in your marriage, we want to suggest you use a different devise. We want you to consider measuring your time in terms of its value. In other words, how valuable is the time you spend together? After all, each of us places a different value on the increments of time, as the following reveals:

To know the value of *one year* . . .
        ask the student who failed the final exam.
To know the value of *one month* . . .
        ask the mother of a premature baby.
To know the value of one week . . .
        ask the editor of a weekly newsmagazine.

To know the value of *one day* . . .
>ask the wage earner who has six children.

To know the value of *one hour* . . .
>ask the lovers who are waiting to meet.

To know the value of *one minute* . . .
>ask the person who missed the plane.

To know the value of *one second* . . .
>ask the person who survived the accident.

To know the value of *one millisecond* . . .
>ask the Olympic silver medalist.

When you begin to measure time in terms of its value, rather than how many minutes or hours have passed, it helps you put it into perspective. Rather than thinking about where you can carve out an hour together in your schedules, you can begin to think in terms of what you'd like that hour to accomplish for you. Maybe what you really want is a time to share a good laugh, or a time to be known, or a time to solve a particular problem. And any one of these may take more or less than an hour.

Get the point? Rather than measuring time in increments, try measuring your time in terms of its purpose and you'll be amazed to find you have more time than you thought.

There is a time for everything,
    and a season for every activity
        under heaven.

Ecclesiastes 3:1

Ticked Off

Anger blows out the lamp of the mind.
Robert Green Ingersoll

On a trip to London we visited the "war rooms" where Winston Churchill worked safely underground during World War II. While there we learned that the bombs dropped during this war are still killing people in Europe. They turn up — and sometimes blow up — at construction sites, in fishing nets, or on beaches fifty years after the guns have fallen silent. Thirteen old bombs exploded in France last year alone. Undetected bombs become more dangerous with time because corrosion can expose the detonator.

What is true of bombs that are not dealt with is also true of unresolved anger. Buried anger explodes when we least expect it. Especially in marriage. Ever feel like you stepped on a buried bomb? It's not uncommon for most couples. And think of all the time we waste on anger. After all, it does little for us most of the time. In fact, anger can become quite contagious and cause couples to be irrational.

Consider the story Billy Martin, former New York Yankees manger, tells about hunting in Texas with baseball star Mickey Mantle at his friend's ranch. When they reached the ranch, Mantle told Martin to wait in the car while he checked with his friend. Mantle's friend quickly gave them permission to hunt, but he asked Mantle a favor. He had a pet mule that was going blind, and he didn't have the heart to put him out of his misery. He asked Mantle to shoot the mule for him. When Mantle came back to the car, he pretended to be angry. He scowled and slammed the door. Martin asked him what was wrong, and Mantle said his friend wouldn't let them hunt. "I'm so mad at that guy," Mantle said, "I'm going out to his barn and shoot one of his mules!" Mantle drove like a maniac to the barn. Martin protested, but Mantle was adamant. "Just watch me!" he shouted.

When they got to the barn, Mantle jumped out of the car with his rifle, ran inside, and shot the mule. As he was leaving, though, he heard two shots, and he ran back to the car. He saw that Martin had taken out his rifle too. "What are you doing, Martin?" he yelled.

Martin yelled back, face red with anger, "We'll show that son of a gun! I just killed two of his cows!"

Like we said, anger can become dangerously contagious. When you get angry, the probability of your spouse getting angry increases significantly, and visa versa. So what's our point? That anger is almost always a huge time waster in marriage. Does it ever have its place in marriage? That's not an easy answer. Anger is a human emotion and nearly inevitable. So, on the one hand, yes, it has its place. But on the other hand, anger is so rarely used rightly that we're tempted to say no.

Here's how Aristotle put it: "Anybody can become angry — that is easy; but to be angry with the right person, and to the right degree, and at the right time, and for the right purpose, and in the right way — that is not within everybody's power and is not easy."

The key to being angry the "right way" is to insure that you are not using your anger to inflict pain or "pay back evil for evil," as Scripture says (Romans 12:17). In other words that you are not seeking revenge, but leaving that up to God. When you allow this principle to keep your anger in check you are far more likely to reclaim countless moments in your marriage that would otherwise be given over to the ravages of rage and resentment. Consider the last time you, personally, were angry with your partner. Did you inflict pain on your spouse with your anger? If so, how might you better handle an angry situation like that in the future?

A quick-tempered man
does foolish things.

Proverbs 14:17

Give It a Rest

One of the weaknesses of our age is our apparent inability
to distinguish our need from our greed.
Author Unknown

The Treasure of the Sierra Madre is the story of three down-on-their-luck
prospectors and their search for gold in Mexico. At one point in their
search, prospectors Fred, Bob, and Howard are joined by a fourth man.
No sooner had the new prospector arrived then the four are involved in
a gunfight with several bandits. Although the bandits are scared away,
the fourth prospector is killed. The other three approach the body,
which is propped up against a large rock.

Howard (Walter Huston) bends down and removes the dead man's
wallet and some papers. "His name is James Cody; Dallas, Texas. There's
a letter from Dallas too. Must be his home," Howard says, and shows the
others a photo of a woman. One of them remarks, "Not bad." Howard
starts reading, and then Bob takes over.

Dear Jim:

*Your letter just arrived. It was such a relief to get word after so many months of silence. I
realize of course that there aren't any mailboxes that you can drop a letter in out there in
the wild. But that doesn't keep me from worrying about you. Little Jimmy is fine, but he*

misses his daddy almost as much as I do. He keeps asking, "When's Daddy coming home?"
You say if you do not make a real find this time, you will never go again. I cannot begin
to tell you how my heart rejoices at those words, if you really mean them. Now I feel free
to tell you, I've never thought that any material treasure, no matter how great, is worth
the pain of these long separations.

The country is especially lovely this year. It's been a perfect spring: warm rains and hardly
any frost. The fruit trees are all in bloom. The upper orchard looks aflame, and the lower,
like after a snowstorm. Everybody looks forward to big crops. I do hope that you are back
for the harvest. Of course, I'm hoping that you will at last strike it rich. It is high time
for luck to start smiling upon you. But just in case she doesn't, remember, we've already
found life's real treasure.

Forever yours,
Callie

Fred, played by Humphrey Bogart in this 1948 film says, "Well, I guess we better dig a hole for him."

Nothing pulls us further away from our true treasure than an insatiable greed. Jim certainly had a fine wife in Callie but he felt compelled to once again leave home in search of more fortune. It's a common trap, even today. The desire to "strike it rich" has come between many a husband and wife. Sure, we don't go off to cash in on an actual gold rush these days, but we do go off to put in more hours at something for more money that keeps us away from each other. And when we do, we often miss the richness, the fortune that we already have in each other.

Just this week one of our closest couple friends announced that they were down-sizing. They were moving to a smaller home, selling one of their cars and living a simpler life in exchange for more time.

With two small children and another on the way, some might look at them and think it's time to get another job, climb the corporate ladder. But they've decided to give the rat race a rest in exchange for the luxury of more time together.

Of course, it doesn't always take a drastic decision to distinguish our need from our greed. Sometimes a couple can eliminate just one small activity, one obligation, one pursuit, to find the treasure of more time together. It may be as simple as eliminating the extra hour being put in at the office or the business calls that are done after coming home. So the next time you find yourself trading in time together for a "great opportunity" or for more cold cash, consider the plight of ol' Jim and how money-hungry ways caused him to miss out on the true treasure of his marriage.

Godliness with contentment is great gain. People who want to get rich fall into temptation and a trap and into many foolish and harmful desires that plunge men into ruin and destruction.

1 Timothy 6:6, 9

Time Is What You Make It

Where, except in the present, can the eternal be met?
C. S. Lewis

Chuck Colson tells the story of visiting Mississippi's Parchman Prison where he found most of the death row inmates in their bunks wrapped in blankets, staring blankly at little black-and-white TV screens, killing time. But in one cell a man was sitting on his bunk, reading. "As I approached," says Colson, "he looked up and showed me his book — an instruction manual on Episcopal liturgy."

John Irving, on death row for more than fifteen years, was studying for the priesthood. John told Colson he was allowed out of his cell one hour each day. The rest of the time, he studies.

Seeing that John had nothing in his cell but a few books, Colson asked, "Would you like a TV if I could arrange it?"

John smiled gratefully. "Thanks," he said, "but no thanks. You can waste an awful lot of time with those things." For the fifteen years since a judge placed a number on his days, John has determined not to waste the one commodity he had to give to the Lord — his time.

Kind of gives you pause, doesn't it? A prisoner on death row who doesn't have time for television! It can also make you realize that time, wherever you spend it, is truly what you make it.

Sally Cunneen, writing in *The Christian Century*, tells of evaluating her everyday use of time and resources and noticing how often she tended to count and measure — abstracting from a situation rather than living it. "Take the routine of soft-boiling an egg," she writes. "After the water came to a boil — a goal for which I would wait impatiently — I would slowly count to one hundred while the egg cooked to the desired firmness. In this numerical mode, I would keep an eye on the clock and sometimes snap at my husband, absorbed in the newspaper."

After reflecting, Sally tried a new way of measuring the cooking time for eggs — one she would have scorned as a young wife and mother interested in "saving" time. Experimentation showed that the eggs are cooked to perfection after three verses of a hymn. "I watch the water with interest until it boils, then I use the boiling time to place myself in touch with earlier generations of cooks who measured their recipes with litanies, using time to get beyond it."

So what about the two of you? Are you simply passing time when you could be making it better? After all, time is what you make it. Each and every day you have an opportunity to optimize your time. As Arnold Bennet said, "You wake up in the morning with twenty-four hours of the unmanufactured tissue of the universe of your life. It is yours. It is the most precious of possessions. No one can take it from you. It is unstealable. And no one receives either more or less."

So don't allow your next twenty-four hours to pass without making them what you want. And consider how each of you can help each other do just that.

Teach us how short our life is, so that we may become wise.

Psalm 90:12 GNT

Your Finest Hour

Deep within humans dwell those slumbering powers; powers that would astonish them, that they never dreamed of possessing; forces that would revolutionize
their lives if aroused and put into action.
Orison Marden

In April 1970 the spacecraft Apollo 13 was crippled by an in-flight explosion. The astronauts relied on archaic navigational techniques to get back home. A slight miscalculation could have sent the ship spiraling thousands of miles off course into outer space. Even if navigation back into earth's orbit succeeded, fears remained that the heat shield and parachutes were not functional. In addition, a tropical storm was brewing in the landing zone.

At one point, a press agent for NASA asks an official for more information. As the press agent recounts the multitude of dangers facing the crew, the NASA official, clearly stressed, responds, "I know what the problems are. It will be the worst disaster NASA's ever experienced."

A NASA chief overhears this pessimistic assessment and responds sharply, "With all due respect, I believe this is going to be our finest hour."

A mixture of fear and hope etches the faces of the NASA team, friends, and family of the astronauts as they watch for any sign of a successful reentry. Three minutes after the reentry process begins, Walter Cronkite's voice informs the viewing audience that no space capsule has taken longer than three minutes to complete reentry. A NASA employee continues to attempt to contact the Odyssey, saying, "Odyssey, this is Houston. Do you read me?" The silence is agonizing. Suddenly, the receiver at NASA crackles. A capsule seems to materialize out of thin air on the screen, and the parachutes look like giant flowers that have burst into bloom.

A voice responds loud and clear, "Hello, Houston. This is Odyssey. It's good to see you again."

Few would dispute the opinion of the NASA official who said it was their finest hour. After all, the times that test one's mettle are opportunities for the human spirit to shine. That's true not only for organizations like NASA; it's true for marriages too.

Your finest hour is not when everything is going well and you're on easy street. Your finest hour, truly, is when times are tough and you stick it out, fight for your marriage, function under pressure, and make it to the other side — triumphantly.

Good marriages battle bad things, like a game that is won one play at a time or a building that is built brick by brick. Smart couples don't expect the world to fall into their laps. It never has. But somewhere deep in the soul of every marriage, a husband and wife can find what Orison Marden calls their "slumbering powers." And these astonishing powers, when awoken, can rise up, look bad fortune in the face, and begin to revolutionize their relationship. It may be a gradual revolution, but it can be a trust-building, heart-healing, love-renewing revolution, just the same.

So if your marriage has bumped its head on something bad, remember that every revolution begins with a battle. And in the case of marriage, it is a battle against the bad things that have had the audacity to attack love. When you begin to fight that battle, you will experience your finest hour.

Thanks *be* unto God, which always causeth us to triumph in Christ.

2 Corinthians 2:14 KJV

Work, Work, Work

Men tire themselves in pursuit of rest.
Laurence Sterne

Nobody saw it coming. Back in the 1950s, with prosperity on the rise and automated machines marching into the workplace, experts warned of an excess of free time. With computers and other gadgets of connivance, Americans, they thought, were headed into a time of less work and more leisure. Sociologists even founded an institute to prepare for the dangerous glut of leisure time they saw coming.

Well, society's fortune-tellers couldn't have missed the mark more. Today's workforce puts in tirelessly long and hard hours. In the past fifteen years, the typical adult's leisure time has shrunk by 40 percent   down from twenty-six hours a week to sixteen hours a week. The average adult now pumps forty-seven hours per week into work (way above the forty hours logged in 1973). And when it comes to professionals and business owners, the numbers jump to fifty-five hours per week.

No doubt about it. Work is consuming. It is common for people to complain about it and avoid it. Some even call in sick to get out of it. But only a small minority of us say we could do without our jobs. Not just because we need the money, but because we like it.

The work-for-money model passed decades ago. The new American worker is motivated by gratification and fulfillment, not just financial security. Our desire to work, however, has left weekends — the traditional time for leisure and recuperation for couples and families — to be filled with more work: catching up on chores and errands. In fact, most Americans feel no more rested on Sunday night than they did on Friday.

Ask anyone what most robs their marriage of time together and you will hear a one word answer: Work. But why? Why do we allow work to steal our time together? One reason that experts point to is that we too often mistake what we do at work with who we are as people. We hang our worth and significance on it.

When I (Les) was training as a medical psychologist, a well-known, highly respected and honored scientific thinker gave a heady lecture on "the etiology of schizophrenia" for the hospital interns. I don't remember much of the lecture, but I will never forget what he said near the end of his remarks. He turned off the projector, leaned over the podium and made a surprising proclamation to the young scholars who filled the small auditorium: "I was asked to speak to you on my most recent findings and I have done that. Now let me tell you young doctors what I wish someone would have told me when I sat where you are. You can save yourself unnecessary frustration in the course of your careers if you ask yourself why you are doing what you are doing. For more than thirty years I have struggled and strained to make an impact in my field, and some would say I have."

The room was deathly still as he continued. "But only recently have I learned that I cannot measure my self-worth by the number of articles I publish or the number of people who applaud my findings." That was it. He gathered up his lecture notes and sat down. We were stunned. It took time for his mini message to sink in, but there was no denying the fact that he had touched a nerve with this group of hard-driving students.

In his helpful book *Ordering Your Private World*, Pastor Gordon Mac-Donald writes: "A driven person is usually caught in the uncontrolled pursuit of expansion . . . rarely having any time to appreciate the achievements to date. They are usually too busy for the pursuit of ordinary relationships in marriage or family, not to speak of one with God."

What's driving you? Why are you working so hard? If you're like most, you'll say to have more time to rest, more time for leisure, right? Well, maybe it's time to cash in on all your hard work with a little extra time together. What's one specific thing you can do that's work-related this week so that you can enjoy more time together at home?

By wisdom a house is built,
        and through understanding it is established;
through knowledge its rooms are filled
        with rare and beautiful treasures.

Proverbs 24:3–4

I Haven't Got Time for the Shame

A stitch in time would have confused Einstein.
Author Unknown

Anyone who has ever had an airport hassle might be able to identify with Neil Melly's frustration. Melly was in Los Angeles International Airport, attempting to get to Australia, but problems developed when he was unable to purchase a ticket because he lacked a valid credit card.

Most of us might slink away in embarrassment. A flight from LAX to the other side of the world is not small change, and without a credit card, most of us would just go home.

Neil Melly isn't most of us. He ignored that little humiliation and went on to shatter the shame barrier. Hours later, Melly angrily stripped off all his clothes and returned to make a dash for the airport runway. Baggage handlers watched as Melly scaled a fence topped with three strands of barbed wire, fearlessly and without injury. Then Neil sprinted across the tarmac toward a jumbo jet and crawled inside the wheel well.

Most of us might have simply been trying to hide, but Neil Melly picked a plane that was on the move — an Australian plane. The dangers were great. As airport spokeswoman Nancy Castles pointed out, "He could have been sucked up by an engine, or crushed when the landing gear was retracted. And if not he very likely would have frozen to death during the fifteen-and-a-half-hour flight at thirty thousand feet while wearing no clothes."

Pilots stopped the plane, and Melly was coaxed from his hiding place and arrested. The official charge was trespassing. Apparently there's no law against poor problem solving. Or being the butt of jokes.

How we solve problems when things aren't going our way says a great deal about us. Some of us, unlike Melly, are quick to give up. Others of us enjoy a challenge. Many of us are prone to lose our cool under pressure. We might yell or point fingers or smolder with fury. Of course, this doesn't match getting naked and climbing barbed wire, but it's just about as useful.

A biblical proverb (14:17) says, "A quick-tempered man does foolish things." Melly can attest to that. But so can most of us. When we are faced with circumstances that aren't going our way, we become impatient. Our urgency can lead us to do stupid things.

What a shame! Think of all the time we waste when we let urgency get the better of us. Somebody said that urgency blows out the lamp of the mind, and it's true. We rarely do our best thinking when we feel frustrated and pressured. That's why one of the kindest things we can do for each other as husband and wife is to ease each other's urgency. How? By lending a listening ear and serving as a solid sounding board. Let's face it, if Melly's wife had been on hand when he was contemplating how to get to Australia, do you think he would have streaked into the news that fateful day at LAX? Doubtful.

Sure, it's an extreme example, but it makes the point. Marriage provides a built-in mechanism for keeping us sane, if we let it. Think of a time when you were feeling under pressure and made a quick decision or behaved rashly. Wouldn't you have benefited from the objective ears of your spouse? Never take them for granted. They may save you a lot of time, not to mention a lot of shame.

Plans fail for lack of counsel,
but with many advisers they succeed.

Proverbs 15:22

Slow Down,
You Age Too Fast

*A person is always startled when he hears himself seriously
called an old man for the first time.*
Oliver Wendell Homes

What did you have for dinner last night? Where did you park your car
last time you were at the grocery? You probably can't quite remember,
and according to a recent study, it's because everyday routines cause our
brains to click to autopilot, making the days seem to pass more quickly.

Dinah Avni-Babad, a psychologist at the Hebrew University in
Jerusalem, found that while we rarely remember routine actions, new
experiences become more embedded in our memories. Even though
it seems counterintuitive, routine is a form of inaction, she says.
"When you tell people routine makes things go faster they say, 'Hmm.
Can't be.'"

It helps to think of routine as a straight line in one's memory, she
explains. New experiences cause the line to be jagged, packed with new
perceptions. This "straight-line" effect accounts for the old adage that
time passes more quickly as we age. We simply encounter fewer new

experiences as we grow older. "The days feel much, much longer when you're a child,' she says. Want time to pass more slowly? Shake up your life, suggests Avni-Babad. Get out of your rut and try something new.

Of course, that's not always as easy as it sounds. Some of us are stuck in a rut because we like it. We don't have to think about much when we are in our routine. But that's the point! Because we're not thinking about it time slips by more rapidly.

To illustrate how inane we can become when stuck in a rut, we want to point out that the U.S. standard railroad gauge is four feet, eight and one-half inches. How did we wind up with such an odd railway width? Because that was the width English railroad-building expatriates brought with them to America. Why did the English build them this wide? Because the first British rail lines were built by the same people who built the pre-railroad tramways, and that's the gauge they used. Why did they use that gauge? Because the same jigs, tools, and people who built wagons built the tramways and used the standard wagon-wheel spacing. Wagon-wheel spacing was standardized due to a very practical, hard-to-change, and easy-to-match reality. When Britain was ruled by Imperial Rome, Roman war chariots, in true bureaucratic fashion, all used a standard spacing between their wheels.

Over time, this spacing left deep ruts along the extensive road network the Romans built. If British wheel spacing didn't match Roman ruts, the wheels would break. The Roman standard was derived after trial-and-error efforts of early wagon and chariot builders. They determined the best width that would accommodate two horses was four feet, eight and one-half inches. Thus, the U.S. standard railroad gauge is a hand-me-down standard based on the original specification for an Imperial Roman war chariot.

Can you believe it? All because we didn't want to have to think about it, because we wanted to do what was easiest in the moment, we ended up with something that would never have been what we would have chosen today. And that happens in many marriages time and again — if we don't take deliberate actions to get out of our ruts and spice up our existence.

It's a little-known fact that you can slow down time in your relationship by doing something new. So give it a try. What can the two of you do this week that will get you out of your routine?

The LORD says,
"See, I am doing a new thing! Now it springs up; do you not perceive it?

Isaiah 43:19

Life in the Fast Lane

Runnin' on empty, runnin' blind. I'm runnin' into the sun, but I'm runnin' behind.

Jackson Browne

Dale Rooks, a school crossing guard in Florida, tried everything to get cars to slow down through the school zone where he was in charge. But nothing worked. Not until he took a blow dryer and wrapped it in electrical tape, making it look like a radar gun.

The next day Dale just pointed the thing at cars and, incredibly, drivers began to slam on their breaks. "It's almost comical," Dale said. "It's amazing how well it works."

Dale's clever idea got us thinking about what it would take to get people to slow down in general — not just in their cars. What if your spouse could hold up a radar gun when you were falling victim to hurry sickness? On a day when you were particularly rushed and busy, he or she could clock your speed and pull you over for a little respite. Wouldn't that be convenient?

It's all wishful thinking, we know. But it does give one pause to consider how we might help each other slow down. Jonathan Turnbough tells the story of his mother who was driving his sisters and him to school one day when she was pulled over by a policeman for speeding. After things were worked out with the officer, his mom took off again. She was being very careful to stay under the speed limit. After a few minutes had passed, they all started hearing a strange noise coming from their vehicle "What's that noise?" his mother asked. Laughing, he replied, " That's the sound of slow. We've never heard it before!"

What does slow sound like in your marriage? Seriously, what does it sound like and look like? Chances are one of you is currently wanting the other to slow down or maybe both of you realize you've got to ease up on your pace. Many couples will say, "We've just got to slow down." Okay. But what does that look like in tangible terms? In other words, how will you know when you've slowed down?

For us, a sure sign of slowing down means both of us being home with our boys for an evening with nothing scheduled past five o'clock, except time together. It also means not holding phone conferences while driving in the car with the rest of the family present. It means being able to take our little ones to the park without a time limit. And the sound of slowness in our home means hearing casual conversation around the dinner table. It means hearing the waves on the beach in our neighborhood while we're taking in the sunset together.

So we'll ask you again. What are the sounds and sights of slow in your relationship? Answering this question just might help you find more of them.

Jesus said, "Come to me, all you who are weary and burdened, and I will give you rest. Take my yoke upon you and learn from me, for I am gentle and humble in heart, and you will find rest for your souls."

Matthew 11:28 – 29

Your Top Time-Saving Device

Time management is really a misnomer—the challenge is not to manage time, but to manage ourselves.
Stephen R. Covey

A minister, a boy scout, and a computer executive were flying to a meeting in a small, private plane. About halfway to their destination, the pilot came back and announced that the plane was going to crash and that there were only three parachutes and four people.

The pilot said, "I am going to use one of the parachutes because I have a wife and four small children," and he jumped.

The computer executive said, "I should have one of the parachutes because I am the smartest man in the world and my company needs me," and he jumped.

The minister turned to the Boy Scout and, smiling sadly, said, "You are young and I have lived a good, long life, so you take the last parachute and I'll go down with the plane."

The Boy Scout said, "Relax, Reverend, the smartest man in the world just strapped on my backpack and jumped out of the plane!"

A high IQ has never guaranteed good decisions.

No matter how superior one's intelligence, even a genius may not recognize the obvious. One need not look far to find breathtaking acts of stupidity committed by people who are smart. You may be quick-witted, clever, and intellectually brilliant, but these enviable traits don't ensure wise judgments. Especially when it comes to saving time.

Most people, no matter how intelligent, seem to neglect their top time-saving device. They seem to wander through their days allowing their schedules to swallow their time — as if they don't have a choice. You see, making a choice is your secret weapon in combating time stealers. Once you realize that you are in charge of your time, you can begin to do something about it.

Now we can almost hear you saying "No duh!" We agree. It's so obvious that it seems ridiculous to even say it. But then why are so many smart people living with out-of-control schedules and complaining about the speed of their life as they rush from one thing to the next? Because they've ignored their Time IQ. They live as if they don't have a choice. But they do. We all do.

"You can't do anything about the length of your life," said Evan Esar, "but you can do something about its width and depth." You can choose how you spend the days you have. You can choose to live them on fast-forward or you can choose to press pause from time to time.

This is all a way of saying that you alone are responsible for what you choose to do and when you do it. If you are feeling like your time is wall to wall, don't look to blame anyone. Make a new choice.

We shape our lives, not to mention our schedules, by the choices we make. This begs the question: What choice can you make, right now, to create the pace you long for? What activity can you choose to lop off your schedule? What day or time can you choose to reserve and protect just for the two of you? "When you have to make a choice and you don't make it," said William James, "that is in itself a choice. So the question is not whether you, individually, and as a couple, have a choice — each one of us has this inherent time-saving device within our reach — but what will your choice be?

I have set before you life and death,
blessings and curses.
Now choose life, so that you and
your children may live.

Deuteronomy 30:19

From Generation to Generation

A family is a place where principles are hammered and honed on the anvil of everyday living.

Charles R. Swindoll

What do you know about your grandparents' marriage? Your great-grandparents' marriage? Of course you know plenty about your mom and dad's relationship. After all, it was your model for marriage growing up. Whether it was happy or sad, or nearly nonexistent, you observed it up close and personal.

All of us take something from the previous generation's example of marriage into our own. It's inevitable. We may even resist some aspect of our parents' marriage and then find ourselves doing the very same thing. We psychologists call this an *introject* — it's kind of like getting injected with ways of being from our family of origin. And this process can offer both good and bad character qualities. But make no mistake; we are all inextricably linked to our families' lineage.

Consider this telling poem about the passage of time through the generations:

When I was a little lad, my old grandfather said
That none should wind the clock but he, and so at time for bed
I le'd fumble for the curious key kept high upon the shelf
And set aside that little task entirely for himself.
In time, Grandfather passed away and so that duty fell
Unto my father who performed the weekly custom well.
He held that clocks were not to be by careless persons wound
And he alone should turn the key or move the hands around.
I envied him that little task and wished that I might be
The one entrusted with the turning of the key.
But year by year the clock was his exclusive bit of care
Until the day the angels came and smoothed his silver hair.
Today the task is mine to do, like those who've gone before.
I am a jealous guardian of that round and glassy door.
And until, at my chamber door, God's messenger shall knock,
To me alone shall be reserved the right to wind the clock.

From generation to generation we are handed responsibilities and qualities that keep the customs going — whether we know it or not. So take a moment to explore what you brought into your marriage from your bloodline. Simply talking about this "relational inheritance" will make it more conscious and shed light on your current conditions.

What character qualities were handed off to you by virtue of the parents and grandparents you have? Consider your family's positive qualities as well as your family's inevitable shortcomings. If you were to diagram a family tree of strengths and weaknesses what would yours look like?

"The family is the country of the heart," said Giuseppe Mazzini. And exploring your spouse's country is always a grand adventure that is sure to join your hearts together. So take a few minutes, right now, to do just that. After all, life is ticking and there's no time like the present. Literally.

Ruth said, "Where you go I will go, and where you stay I will stay. Your people will be my people and your God my God."

Ruth 1:16

Conclusion

Every thread of gold is valuable, so is every minute of time.
John Mason

We've got a confession to make. We're busy. Sometimes hurried and harried. We feel the pressure of impending deadlines. We live in a time-conscious household in the city of Seattle with two little boys and a jam-packed schedule. But that's not our confession. That's life.

The confession is that we wrote this book for us as much as we did for you. When we wrote our book *The Time-Starved Marriage*, we wanted a tool for our own marriage that we could use weekly to get us to slow down and reconnect with one another. So as we wrote the words you've read in the mediations of this little book, we want you to know that we've done our best to practice what we preach. And along the way we've found something to be true for us that may be true for you.

As the two of us would ponder each of the mediations in this book, we sometimes felt as though we were "shoe-horning" them into our lives, like we were forcing it. "There, we've had our 'time together,'" kind of idea. "Now we can check that off our list and get back to the real tasks at hand." Did you ever feel that way as you were going through these pages together?

If so, that's okay. Because what we also found is that the effort, even if it was very little, seemed to make a big difference. In the process of writing and later reading these meditations together, we found that we had created more space for our relationship in our lives. In fact, we've come to call these little meditations our "penny moments." Why? Well, because pennies are a dime a dozen, so to speak. Without much effort, one could find a penny on the floor or in a parking lot. And without much effort you can spend five minutes at some point in your week reading a mediation from this book. No big deal.

Or so it seems.

In truth, these penny moments seem to add up and almost compound when a husband and wife begin to collect them. Just like actual pennies do. For example, did you know that a one-cent-per-case increase of Coca-Cola would bring the company an additional $45 million a year? Or that if Krispy Kreme increased the cost of each donut by one penny, the company would increase profits by $27 million?

It's tough to believe but it's true. And it may seem hard to fathom that the few minutes you've spent over the past few weeks in reading through this little book could have much payoff. But we believe it will. And we wish you every success and joy as you continue to enjoy time together.

"The LORD bless you
and keep you;
the LORD make his face shine upon you
and be gracious to you;
the LORD turn his face toward you
and give you peace."

Numbers 6:24

About the Authors

Drs. Les and Leslie Parrott are co-directors of the Center for Relationships Development at Seattle Pacific University (SPU), a groundbreaking program dedicated to teaching the basics of good relationships. Les Parrott is a professor of clinical psychology at SPU, and Leslie is a marriage and family therapist at SPU. The Parrotts are authors of the Gold Medallion Award-wining *Saving Your Marriage Before It Starts*, *Becoming Soul Mates*, *The Love List*, *Relationships*, and *When Bad Things Happen to Good Marriages*. They have been featured on *Oprah*, *CBS This Morning*, *CNN*, and *The View*, and in *USA Today* and the *New York Times*. They are also frequent guest speakers and have written for a variety of magazines. The Parrotts radio program, *Love Talk*, can be heard on stations throughout North America. They live in Seattle, Washington, with their two sons. Visit their website at *www.RealRelationships.com*.

More books from Drs. Les and Leslie Parrott

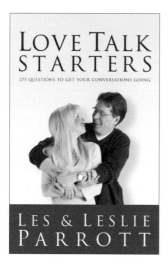

Love Talk Starters

ISBN 0-310-81047-7

In this book you will find engaging, intriguing, and revealing conversation starters. Some questions are just for fun, some will educate you about your spouses's life, and still others will drill down on some more serious topics. Use these simple conversation starters and begin communicating your way into a happier, healthier, and stronger relationship today.

Just the Two of Us

ISBN 0-310-80381-0

Filled with personal stories, carefully selected Scriptures, and inspirational quotations, this beautiful keepsake book will encourage couples to speak each other's language as they never have before.

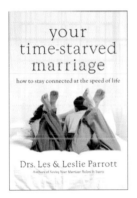

Your Time-Starved Marriage

ISBN 0-310-24597-4

This is not a book about being more productive—it's a book about being more connected. Drs. Les and Leslie Parrott show you how you can create a more fulfilling relationship with time—and with each other.

Visit *www.realrelationships.com* for more marriage insights.

At Inspirio, we'd love to hear
your stories and your feedback.
Please send your comments to us
by way of email at
icares@zondervan.com
or to the address below:

inspirio

Attn: Inspirio Cares
5300 Patterson Avenue SE
Grand Rapids, MI 49530

If you would like further information
about Inspirio and the products we
create, please visit us at:
www.inspiriogifts.com

Thank You and God bless!